which paintbrush would be the last one left on the board? It's not as easy as it looks!

....

....

is having an ART AttACK!

ART ATTACK

ANNUAL 2001

A DORLING KINDERSLEY BOOK

Dorling **DK** Kindersley

LONDON, NEW YORK, SYDNEY, DELHI, PARIS,
MUNICH and JOHANNESBURG

Project Editor Selina Wood
Senior Art Editor Carole Oliver
Designer Jacqueline Gooden

Model Maker Jim Copley
Photography Steve Gorton, Gary Ombler, Stephen Oliver
Illustration Dorian Spencer Davies

Managing Editor Mary Ling
Managing Art Editor Rachael Foster
Production Orla Creegan
DTP Designer Almudena Díaz
Jacket Designer Dean Price

Published in Great Britain in 2000 by
Dorling Kindersley Limited
9 Henrietta Street, London, WC2E 8PS
2 4 6 8 10 9 7 5 3 1

Copyright © 2000 Dorling Kindersley Limited
Art Attack TM retained by The Media Merchants TV Co. Ltd

Colour reproduction by GRB Editrice S.r.l., Verona, Italy
Printed and bound in China by L. Rex

Dorling Kindersley would like to thank everyone at
Media Merchants for their help and enthusiasm.
www.artattack.co.uk

see our complete
catalogue at
www.dk.com

CONTENTS

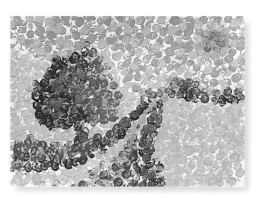

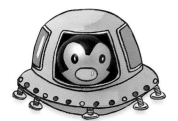

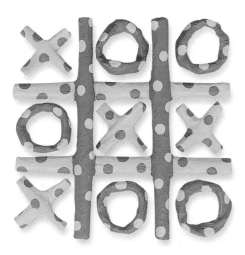

INTRODUCTION

Hi there! Welcome to the very first Art Attack Annual – full of lots more fantastic art ideas and terrific 3-D projects that are guaranteed to turn you into an artist. And there's lots more great stuff in this book. You can take a look behind the scenes at the Art Attack studio and get involved in the action as we put a programme together. And if you want to get all the inside information about me, turn to Spotlight on Neil on pages 32-33. Plus, there are some brilliant brainteasers and quizzes, a magical maze, and some fantastic 3-D puzzles. So, have fun and remember that you don't have to be good at art to create amazing Art Attacks! Try them yourself – grab your pencils and paints, and have an Art Attack!

Neil Buchanan

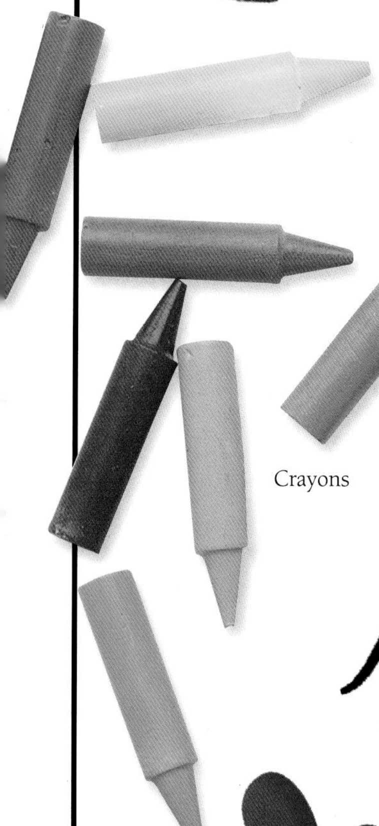

PVA glue

Crayons

Marker pens

Coloured chalks

8

Acrylic paint

Paint

You will need three different kinds of paint for the projects in this annual: acrylic, poster, and watercolour. Use a palette or old plate to mix your colours.

Paint palette

Hints and tips

- Make sure you open the windows when you use marker pens.
- Thick cardboard is easier to cut if you wet it slightly with water.
- Emphasize details on your models by outlining them in thick, black marker pen.
- A balloon pump is a quick and easy way to blow up balloons.
- When you sprinkle glitter over a project, lay a piece of paper underneath so that you can pour excess glitter back into the pot.

Split pins

Sticky tack

Sticky tape

Protractor

Lolly stick

Pencil

Fine marker pen

Paintbrush

Ruler

Scissors

Kitchen towel and toilet paper

Sticky-backed plastic

Kitchen foil

Glitter

Cardboard

Use different size plates as templates for perfect circles.

White card

Coloured paper

Newspaper

Poster paint

9

ON THE SET

Ever wondered how an Art Attack programme is put together? Join me here in the studio and find out the secrets . . .

The set
Enter the world of giant glue pots and pink and orange paint splats. These props make up the Art Attack set where we film the programme. The set is part of a larger recording area known as a studio.

The script
Here I'm checking my lines standing by my "secret desk". This is where I keep my script, a glass of water, and a pair of dark glasses.

Action!
I rehearse each Art Attack a few times, and when everyone is ready we start to record. Here I am talking away at the camera, mid-Art Attack.

The Art Attack splats are all over the set. How many can you see?

Give me water!
Because it's so hot in the studio, I get thirsty quickly and have to drink loads of water. You may wonder why I'm wearing super-cool dark glasses. This is to stop the bright studio lights from giving me a headache!

Voilà!
Sometimes we film for 15 continuous minutes while I complete a whole painting from start to finish. This is one of many finished works of art that I have at the end of a busy day of filming.

We had great fun deciding which art tools to blow up for the Art Attack set!

Although these massive paintbrushes look real, they don't work for my Big Art Attacks!

ART ATTACK DRAWING PAD

BEHIND THE SET

Let me show you what the studio looks like from behind my art desk. You can see the skilled team of people working away behind the scenes to bring about an Art Attack programme.

Floor cameras
Three camera operators film me as I make an Art Attack. Two of the cameras are located at floor level and film me from the front as I move around on the set.

The aerial camera moves up, out of the way, when it is not in use.

Lighting
The studio lights have to be very strong and bright so that the images we record are clear. Lighting technicians with sophisticated equipment check that the light level is just right.

The camera operator wears headphones, which enable him to hear instructions from the director.

The vital ingredients for an Art Attack... cameras, light and sound technicians, a director, all the art gear, oh, and I nearly forgot... me!

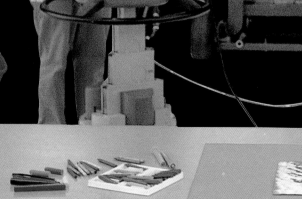

Aerial camera

The aerial camera records from above so that you, the viewer, can watch my hands working on the Art Attack. A camera operator works the aerial camera from the studio floor and uses a joystick to control its movement. I can see the angle of my hands on my monitor.

Mixing gallery

Our director watches what we are recording in the gallery and can talk to the team via microphones. The director decides what image should appear on the screen, a vision mixer blends the images that come in from three cameras, and an editor copies all the best bits on to a tape ready for broadcast.

Monitor

When I am being filmed on the aerial camera, I can sometimes obscure the camera's view if I lean over to draw. Therefore I have to lift my head up and watch my monitor to see what I'm drawing. Tricky!

Both floor cameras film at the same time and the director will choose which shot will be used for the broadcast.

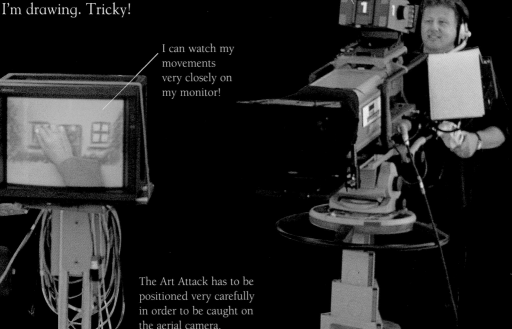

I can watch my movements very closely on my monitor!

The Art Attack has to be positioned very carefully in order to be caught on the aerial camera.

Sound

My voice is recorded with a tiny microphone that I wear disguised on my sweatshirt. It has to be absolutely quiet in the studio when we film – any laughing or coughing is picked up by the studio microphones!

PAPIER POWER

Papier-mâché is a brilliant material for moulding 3-D models. Here are some helpful tips and ideas for generating papier-mâché power!

You will need

1 part water (e.g. one tablespoon)

2 parts PVA glue (e.g. two tablespoons – twice as much as the water)

Strips of kitchen towel or newspaper

How to make papier-mâché

Prepare your glue mixture by adding one part water to every two parts PVA glue. Tear up some strips of loo roll, kitchen towel, or newspaper. Cover your model with glue mixture, and lay the strips on top. As you build up layers, keep adding more glue mixture on top with a paintbrush. You will need at least three layers on the model and don't worry about it getting messy – when it has dried overnight it will be stiff and rock hard!

Balloon base

Balloons are a great base for making head-shaped models. Just add four layers of newspaper papier-mâché and when the mould is dry, you can pop the balloon. You are then left with an oval mould. If you want to add facial features to a papier-mâché mask, mould them from a pulp mixture of tissue and PVA glue.

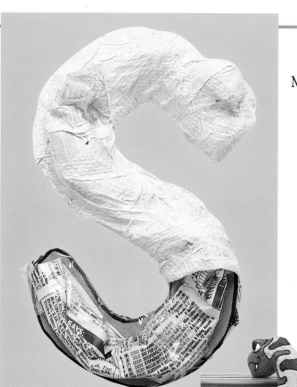

Funny face bowl

Make your own colourful bowl by adding papier-mâché to the inside of a breakfast or soup bowl. To make it easy to separate the mould from the bowl, first cover the inside of the bowl with cling wrap. When the mould is dry, pull the bowl away from the cling wrap.

Cardboard-based snake hook

By using a base of cardboard and newpaper you can create practically any shape you like. This snake hook is made from a cardboard S shape padded out with scrunched up newspaper. Create eyes by rolling up two small newspaper balls. Then add four layers of papier-mâché mixture to mould it into shape.

Newspaper bracelets

Make a jazzy bracelet by adding papier-mâché mixture to a ring of twisted-up newspaper. When it is dry, paint your bracelet with bright or metallic colours.

Building up your papier-mâché

Why not use a combination of different bases to make a mega model like this dinosaur money bank? This uses a balloon base for the body, cardboard for the legs, and newspaper for the neck and tail. Keep experimenting to perfect your papier-mâché!

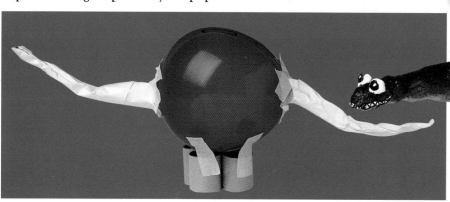

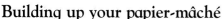

NUMBER PLATE

Ever noticed how number plates sometimes spell out words? Try making your own plates that you can fasten onto your bike.

From card to plate

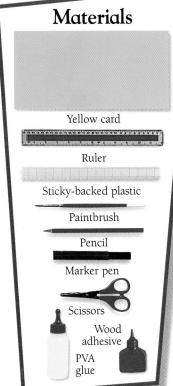

Materials

Yellow card

Ruler

Sticky-backed plastic

Paintbrush

Pencil

Marker pen

Scissors

Wood adhesive

PVA glue

1 Take a large piece of yellow card. With a ruler and pencil draw a 30-cm x 10-cm rectangle. In capital letters, write your name or message inside the rectangle.

Draw two screw holes at each end of the number plate to make it look real.

2 To make the plate waterproof, carefully cover the card with sticky-backed plastic, making sure that you spread it on smoothly. Take care to get rid of any air bubbles.

Hold the sticky-backed plastic down as you spread it across the card slowly.

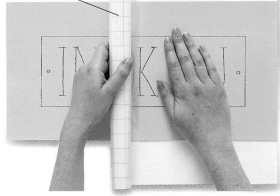

Make your letters big so that they can be seen from a distance.

3 Ask an adult to help you squeeze a layer of wood adhesive over the pencil lines. Leave it to dry overnight.

The marker pen dries with a shiny finish.

4 Take a permanent marker pen and colour over all the hardened adhesive areas in black. This will create the effect of raised lettering that you find on real number plates.

Cut the number plate out carefully with scissors.

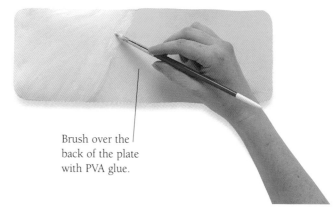

Brush over the back of the plate with PVA glue.

5 Now you are ready to cut the number plate out. With a pair of scissors, cut around the black border, making sure you don't cut into the adhesive layer.

6 Using a brush, cover the back of the plate with a thick layer of PVA glue. This makes the back of the plate stiffer. Let the glue dry.

Colour crazy!

Why not write your name or make up some cryptic messages to go on your number plate? Then you can carefully tie it to the handlebars of your bicycle.

Gold and silver pens create a brilliant, glitzy effect!

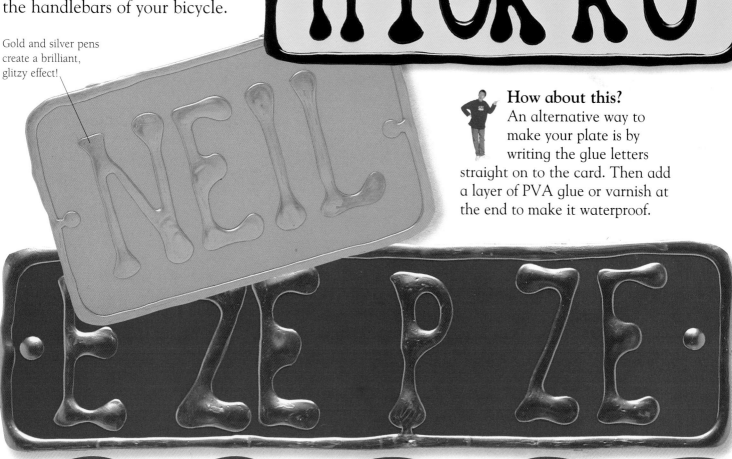

How about this?

An alternative way to make your plate is by writing the glue letters straight on to the card. Then add a layer of PVA glue or varnish at the end to make it waterproof.

FANCY FOOTWORK

How would you like your favourite football players springing to life from your ceiling? Try these fantastic springy-limbed mobiles!

From strips to springs

Fold the bottom strip up over the top strip.

Make sure the strips are exactly the same size.

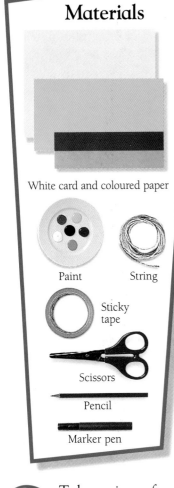

Materials

White card and coloured paper

Paint

String

Sticky tape

Scissors

Pencil

Marker pen

1 Take two pieces of different coloured paper and cut a thin, long strip from each one. Place one strip across the other to form an 'L' shape and tape them together with sticky tape.

2 Fold the paper strips over each other, until you get to the end. Fix the ends together with sticky tape. Repeat steps one and two until you have four springy strips.

Hands are very difficult to draw. If you have trouble, try drawing them with the fists clenched.

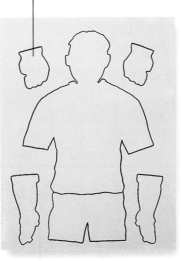

Use the colours of your favourite football team on the T-shirt.

3 Take a piece of white card and draw a body, two hands, and two legs below the knee. The bottom of the sleeves and shorts, the wrists, and the top of the socks should be the same width as the paper springs.

4 Cut out the pieces and decorate them using marker pens or paints. Colour both sides so that when you hang them up it doesn't matter which way they face. Leave them to dry overnight.

You may need quite a few pieces of sticky tape to attach them firmly.

5 Attach the hands and legs to each springy limb with sticky tape. If you want the limbs to be longer, you could always make some extra lengths with more strips and then attach them together.

Attach a piece of string to the back of the head with some tape.

Try making some 3-D hair out of some coloured paper.

6 When your springy limbs are ready, it's time to put your footballer together! Use sticky tape to attach the limbs to the arms and the shorts. Ensure that they are fixed securely.

Main man
Every footballer needs a ball to keep them occupied! Draw the shape of a ball on white card, cut it out, and attach it to a foot with sticky tape.

Team players
Why not create an entire team with their own names and numbers on their shirts? Hang them in your room and watch them spring!

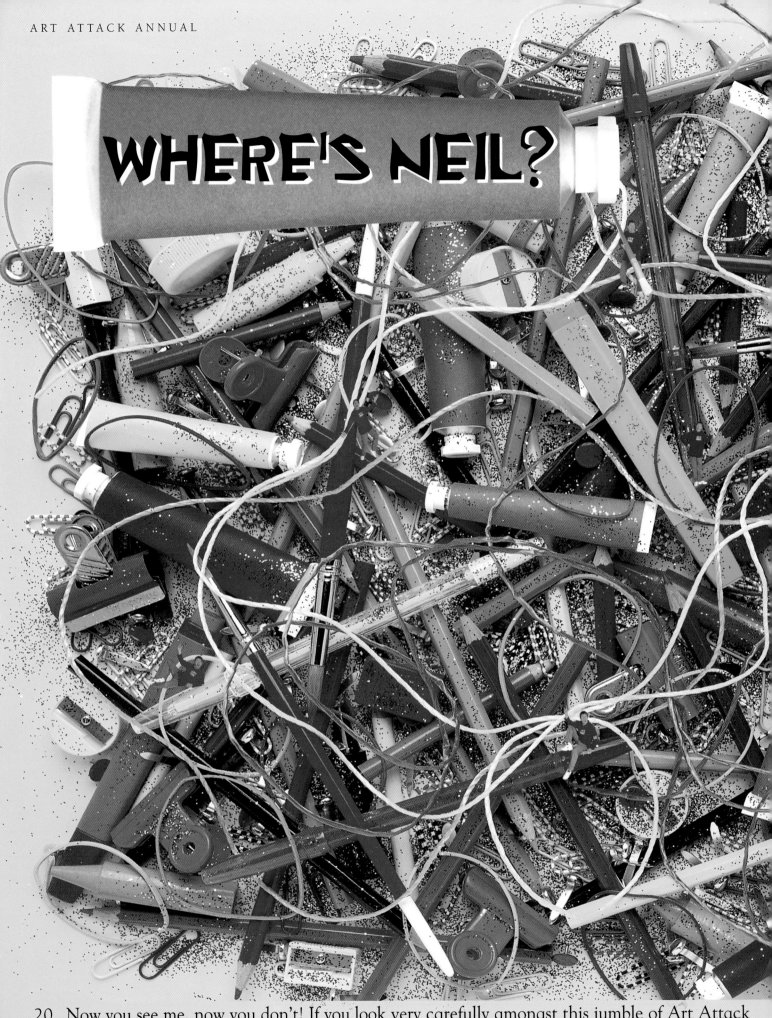

WHERE'S NEIL?

20 Now you see me, now you don't! If you look very carefully amongst this jumble of Art Attack

materials, you will find ten little pictures of me. Find me if you can – happy Neil-hunting!   21

ALL CHANGE

Here's a clever way to create a picture that changes from day to night in a flash. It's easy to make, and will amaze your friends!

From card to picture

Draw around a plate with a pencil.

Mark the centre point of each circle with a pencil.

Materials

Thick paper or thin card

Plate

Split pin

Paints

Sticky tack

Scissors

Ruler

Pencil

Paintbrush

Marker pen

Metallic pen

1 Take a piece of thick paper or thin card, and a plate. Turn the plate upside-down and draw around it to make two circles. Cut them out.

2 Using a ruler and pencil, measure across each circle to find the centre. With a pencil, pierce a hole through the centre point.

Placing some sticky tack underneath, pierce a hole in the centre of each circle.

Colour in your picture with paints or marker pens.

Draw lines across the area you'll want to cut out.

3 Take one of the circles and draw a wavy horizontal line just above the centre point. This will be the horizon line for your landscape scene.

4 Draw some features, such as a house, on the horizon line. Add a landscape scene underneath. Then cut out the sky above the horizon line.

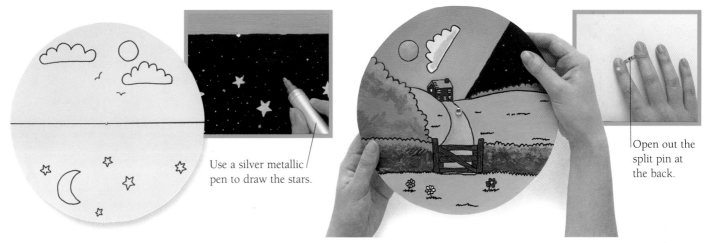

Use a silver metallic pen to draw the stars.

Open out the split pin at the back.

5 Draw a line through the centre of your second circle. In the top half, draw a sun and some clouds, and in the bottom section, stars and a moon. Colour it with paints and metallic pens.

6 Place your landscape picture over your sky picture and push a split pin through the centre hole of both circles. Open out the split pin at the back. Now you just twirl around your picture to change day into night.

Twirl pictures

All change! See how different the landscapes look when you change the sky around. Use lots of bright, bold colours to make other fantastic pictures such as cityscapes or jungle scenes.

Use a black marker pen to add detail.

Paint large images in the foreground so that the picture jumps out at you!

Sunshine and showers

Try creating pictures where you can change the weather. Experiment with rainbows, lightning, typhoons – anything you feel like!

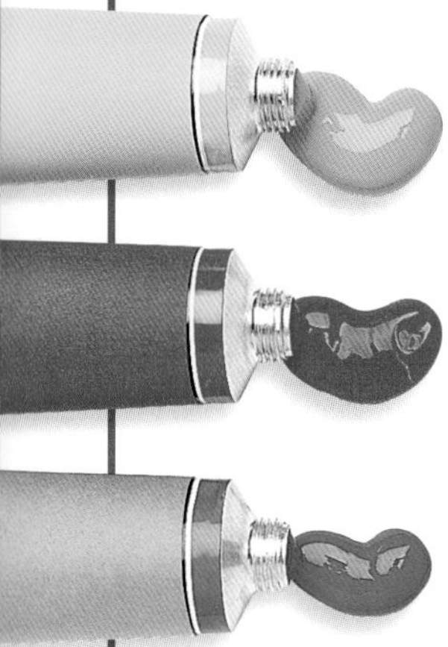

PAINT EFFECTS

Have you noticed all the different types of paints you can buy? There are brilliant things you can do with them, and that doesn't just mean painting pictures!

Wax scraping with paint

You can create very striking pictures using paint and wax crayon. Cover a piece of paper with lots of colours in crayon. Next, mix some black poster paint with an equal amount of washing-up liquid. Brush the mixture over the page and leave it to dry. Then scrape out your picture with a cocktail stick. You could also use an old biro or pencil.

Multi-colours look great in wax scraping pictures.

Try pouring two colours into the eggshell. You can create even better "plop" effects!

The best thing about wax scraping is that you never know what colour will appear next!

"Plops" away!

This paint technique is great fun! Make a 2-cm hole in an egg using a spoon handle, as if you were opening a boiled egg. Empty the contents and pour poster paint into the hole. Then, go into the garden and lay out some paper. Hold the egg high over the paper and. . . "plop" away!

Splatter effect

Start by making a stencil. Draw the shape of an animal on some coloured paper and cut it out leaving the outside in one piece. Place the stencil over some white paper. Then dip a toothbrush into some watered-down poster paint. Pull the bristles back and splatter the paint so that tiny drops land on the white paper.

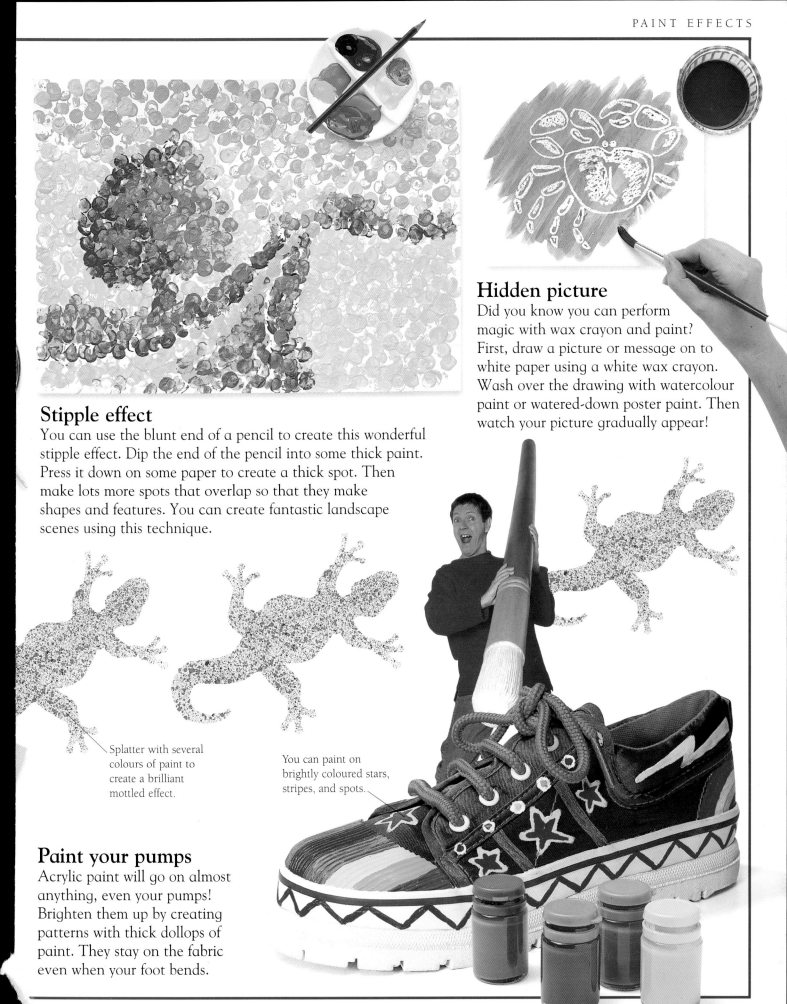

Stipple effect

You can use the blunt end of a pencil to create this wonderful stipple effect. Dip the end of the pencil into some thick paint. Press it down on some paper to create a thick spot. Then make lots more spots that overlap so that they make shapes and features. You can create fantastic landscape scenes using this technique.

Hidden picture

Did you know you can perform magic with wax crayon and paint? First, draw a picture or message on to white paper using a white wax crayon. Wash over the drawing with watercolour paint or watered-down poster paint. Then watch your picture gradually appear!

Splatter with several colours of paint to create a brilliant mottled effect.

You can paint on brightly coloured stars, stripes, and spots.

Paint your pumps

Acrylic paint will go on almost anything, even your pumps! Brighten them up by creating patterns with thick dollops of paint. They stay on the fabric even when your foot bends.

LOLLY LETTERING

Here's a cheap and easy way to really improve your handwriting. All you need is a lolly stick and some ink to become a calligraphy wizard.

From letters to calligraphy

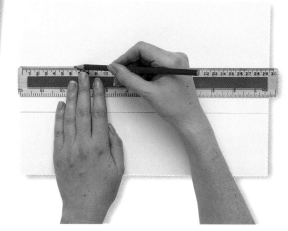

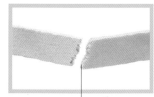

Watch out for any sharp bits when you snap your lolly stick.

1 With a ruler, draw a line across a piece of paper. Pencil in another line along the bottom of the ruler. Move the ruler 1.5–2 cm up and draw a third line.

2 Save the stick from your favourite ice lolly and very carefully snap the stick in half. You may need to get an adult to help you.

Materials

Paper

Ruler

Pencil

Inks

Lolly sticks

Scissors

Marker pen

Just dip the very end of the lolly stick into the ink.

Keep your lolly stick straight as if you were using a fountain pen.

3 Dip the broken end of one of the lolly sticks into some fountain pen ink or some poster paint mixed with lots of water.

4 Keeping the square end of the lolly stick flat on the paper, practise writing with the lolly stick. Try out different effects by altering the length and width of the strokes.

5 Sometimes when you snap a lolly stick you get a jagged edge. Don't throw this away – it can give a good split letter effect. Alternatively, you can create your own jagged edge by snipping bits of the lolly stick away with scissors.

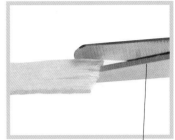

Use a pair of scissors to split the end of your lolly stick.

Calligraphy set

If you snap a lot of sticks you can make a whole set of calligraphy pens that create different styles of lettering. By snipping a notch out of the middle of the end of your stick you can create this fantastic double-lined effect.

Why not make a label to go on your bedroom door?

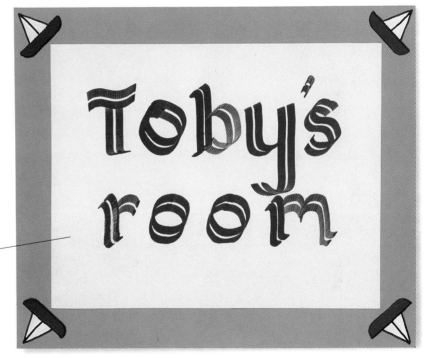

Posh letters

You can make some wonderful notices with your calligraphy set. Frame your notice by placing it on to coloured card and then drawing a frame around it with a marker pen.

Try writing capital letters with your lolly stick.

FACT ATTACK

Did you know that the most famous Art Attacks in history are often the most outlandish? Here are some amazing arty-facts that will turn you into a real art expert.

Brolly good show!
Christo's landscape artwork, *The Umbrellas*, involved the opening of 31,000 umbrellas in Japan and the USA.

At the expense of . . .
Van Gogh's *Portrait of Dr Gachet* sold for a huge £46.1 million after his death. Unfortunately, he only sold one painting in his lifetime.

Get the picture?
In 1961 Henri Matisse's painting *Le Bateau* hung upside-down in the Museum of Modern Art, New York, for two months. Not one of the 116,000 visitors noticed!

Parrot talk
The famous French artist, Paul Cézanne, taught his parrot to say "Paul Cézanne is a great painter!"

You've been framed!
In 1911, Vincent Peruggia strolled out of the Louvre in Paris with the *Mona Lisa*, the most valuable painting in the world, under his arm. It took two years to retrieve it.

Never-ending story
Did you know that by the time workers finish painting Scotland's Forth Bridge, it's time to begin again?

Spick and spam
At Rhode Island College's first Spam Art Festival, the winning entry was *Stonehenge*, a spam model!

Off the wall
UK artist Alan Whitworth has been sketching Hadrian's Wall for more than 13 years. His sketch will be 73 miles long when he finishes it in 2007.

Yukky yellow
The pigment Indian yellow was once made by heating the urine of cows fed on mango leaves.

SP⭐T THE

At first glance it would appear that the two pages are exactly the same – look again!

DIFFERENCE

If you study the two pictures you will find at least 40 differences. Have fun spotting!

SPOTLIGHT ON NEIL

You've seen the studios and how we make a show, now it's time to turn the spotlight on me! All the things you've always wanted to know – what I did before Art Attack, what my star sign is, where I go on holiday . . .

Q How long have you been presenting Art Attack?

I've been presenting Art Attack for about 10 years but it feels like five minutes – it's gone so quickly! We've just finished our 13th series.

Q How did you get onto the show?

I got onto the show because I invented it. The idea was in a drawer for two years because I didn't actually think it was that good! It was only when I took the idea out and we started working it up that I realized it could work.

Playing in a rock band

Q What did you do before Art Attack?

I was in a rock band before I got into telly. I played heavy rock music and I had very long hair. I was a good guitarist – actually a better guitarist than artist!

My star sign is Libra. I'm sensitive, artistic, and... can't make decisions!

Planning an Art Attack, in one of the early series.

Q Do you make Art Attack projects with your kids at home?

Both my kids are very good at art and I test projects out on them. I also get ideas from the children who send stuff into the show.

Q Do you spend a lot of time preparing for Art Attack?

I think of the ideas six months before recording the show and then pass them on to the team to work on. I write the scripts up, then six months later, when we start to rehearse, I don't remember any of it!

One of my doodles on a train ticket

Q What is your favourite Art Attack?

I like the Art Attacks where I make something useful out of rubbish, such as lolly lettering where I made calligraphy pens out of used lolly sticks. Another favourite is the portrait of HRH The Queen using a quarter of a million pounds. I had to borrow the money of course!

Q What medium do you like working with the most?

I used to draw sketches and caricatures of the people opposite me on the train on the back of my ticket. It was a perfect drawing surface. Now my team order sheets of ticket card to use on the show.

> I really love traditional Sunday roast or curry or chocolate – but not altogether!

Big Art Attack picture of HRH The Queen made up of £10 notes.

Q Have any Art Attacks gone badly wrong?

There have been times when I have nearly completed a Big Art Attack and suddenly a rainstorm has come over and washed everything out. And if it's really windy, the whole team has to lie on top of a Big Art Attack to stop it from blowing away!

Q Who is your favourite artist?

My favourite artist is Walt Disney. He did stuff that everybody enjoys and I love the humour in his characters. He was never a "great artist" but his ideas were fantastic.

Q Where do you like to go on holiday?

I often visit the USA because I used to go there a lot as a musician. I always get lots of inspiration from there. I like the way that in America people aren't restricted and just go for things in a big way. Rather than snapshots, I come back with loads of photos of ideas for Art Attack.

On the beach on holiday

PUZZLE PAGE

How good are you at puzzles? Here are some fabulous Art Attack brainteasers to test you. Answers can be found on page 61.

Take the first letter of each object and solve the anagram.

Using these letters, see if you can make 30 new words.

WORD SEARCH

Search for the following artists' names amongst the jumble of letters. There are ten to find.

- DALI
- DEGAS
- LOWRY
- MATISSE
- MONET
- PICASSO
- REMBRANDT
- TURNER
- VAN GOGH
- WARHOL

E	P	I	C	A	S	S	O	N	Y
S	R	E	N	R	U	T	C	R	D
S	Z	E	I	N	B	Y	W	Z	A
I	G	B	M	C	E	O	G	D	L
T	A	R	J	B	L	K	P	E	I
A	Y	D	K	O	R	M	H	G	B
M	O	N	E	T	U	A	F	A	Z
V	Z	B	J	P	U	W	N	S	C
X	V	A	N	G	O	G	H	D	E
S	B	M	W	A	R	H	O	L	T

WHAT IS IT?

Here is some detail taken from an Art Attack Annual project. Can you work out what this is?

CROSSWORD CLUES

ACROSS

1. _ _ _ _ _ _ mâché
4. Something to write with
5. He says "Try it yourself!"
6. Painting, sculpture, drawing . . . all of these
7. Something to put around a picture
10. A violet-blue colour
13. Do red and yellow make orange?

DOWN

1. Type of paint made with water
2. Something that you sharpen
3. Measuring tool
4. Glue used a lot in Art Attack
7. This amphibian is part of the Annual desk tidy
8. Do this with paints to make a new colour
9. You make strokes with this
10. Put this in your fountain pen
11. Polka _ _ _
12. Type of paint used on a canvas

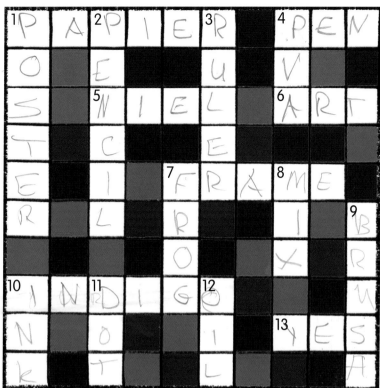

PAINT POT PUZZLE

RPUEPL **NCMOSRI** **IKNP** **TVLIEO**

unscramble the letters to reveal the colours.

DOT·TO·DOT

JOIN THE DOTS TO REVEAL THE PICTURE!

RULES: This is a race through the squiggles and splatters for two or more players.

Players will also come across Art Attack Awards and Neil's Challenges along the way to keep you on your toes.

100 Finish	99	98 Fall back 8 spaces.	97	96 Draw something in 30 seconds. If another player guesses it correctly, everyone moves on 1 space. Art Attack Award
76 Fall back 1 space.	**77**	**78** S	**79** Q	**80** U	**81** I Move on	**82** G
75 Draw something in 30 seconds. If another player guesses it correctly, everyone moves on 2 spaces. Art Attack Award	**74**	**73**	**72** 7TH HEAVEN! Move on 7 spaces.	**71**	**70** You're stuck on a splat! Miss a go.
51	**52** Sharpen 4 pencils in 10 seconds or go back 2 spaces. Neil's Challenge	**53**	**54** Move on	**55** A	**56** N
50 You're stuck on a splat! Miss a go.	**49**	**48** Move on	**47** 7TH HEAVEN! Move on 7 spaces.	**46**	**45**	**44**
26 Draw something in 30 seconds. If another player guesses it correctly, everyone moves on 2 spaces. Art Attack Award	**27**	**28** S	**29** P	**30** L Move on	**31** A T
25	**24** You're stuck on a splat! Miss a go.	**23**	**22** Write your name backwards. If you do it wrong, go back 2 spaces. Neil's Challenge	**21**	**20**
1 Start	**2**	**3** Fall back 1 space.	**4**	**5** You're stuck on a splat! Miss a go.	**6**

PENALTIES: **Stuck on a splat:** miss a turn. **Fall back:** go back the given number of spaces.

36

You will need some counters and a die, pencils, paper, paperclips, a pencil sharpener, and a watch.

| 95 | 94 You're stuck on a splat! Miss a go. | 93 | 92 Make a paper aeroplane. If it doesn't fly, go back 2 spaces. Neil's Challenge | 91 | 90 You're stuck on a splat! Miss a go. |

Players take it in turns to throw the die and move their counters along the spaces on the board.

| 83 G | 84 L | 85 I | 86 E | 87 S 7TH HEAVEN! Move on 7 spaces. | 88 | 89 |

| 69 | 68 | 67 Draw something in 30 seconds. If another player guesses it correctly, everyone moves on 2 spaces. Art Attack Award | 66 | 65 | 64 Fall back 4 spaces. |

| 57 | 58 You're stuck on a splat! Miss a go. | 59 | 60 | 61 Move on | 62 You're stuck on a splat! Miss a go. | 63 |

| 43 D Fall back spaces. | 42 | 41 Draw a recognizable animal with your eyes closed or go back 2 spaces. Neil's Challenge | 40 | 39 | 38 |

| 32 T | 33 E | 34 R | 35 S | 36 Move on | 37 Make a paperclip bracelet in 1 minute or go back 4 spaces. Neil's Challenge |

| 19 You're stuck on a splat! Miss a go. | 18 | 17 | 16 Fall back 3 spaces. | 15 | 14 You're stuck on a splat! Miss a go. | 13 |

| 7 7TH HEAVEN! Move on 7 spaces. | 8 | 9 Move on | 10 | 11 | 12 Draw something in 30 seconds. If another player guesses it correctly, everyone moves on 3 spaces. Art Attack Award |

BONUSES: 7th Heaven: move on 7 squares; **Move on:** follow the paint squiggles to the end.

Press down firmly
to get a clear print.

PRINTING FUN

An easy and effective way to paint lots of shapes that are all the same is by printing. It's a great way to decorate greeting cards and wrapping paper and it's also brilliant fun!

Spectacular spuds

Did you know that you can use potatoes for something a bit more artistic than eating? To make potato prints, first get an adult to help you to cut out a shape from half a large potato using a knife. Then dip the potato shape into some paint and print it on to coloured paper.

❝ Spuds and sponges, feet and string . . . try printing with anything you like!❞

Use bright, bold colour paint on your string.

Add your message in silver pen.

String a daisy

In pencil, draw a simple picture on thick card then cut out pieces of string and glue them on the lines of your drawing. Press the string into a plate of paint and then place it on coloured paper. Try making cool designs for birthday cards with your string prints.

38

Cardboard cut-out

Draw a bold picture, such as this dinosaur scene, on cardboard. Cut out along some of the lines, but leave some outlines in card so that you can still see what the picture is. Stick your cut-out on to another piece of cardboard and add some more details, such as eyes. Cover the image in paint, and print away!

Try and make the silver paint as even as possible.

Make sure you cover your cut-out in a thick layer of paint.

Twinkle little star

For a really glitzy effect, cut out some stars from a sponge and dip them into a plate of silver paint. Print them on to dark-coloured paper to see your stars twinkle! You can make some fantastic, festive wrapping paper using this technique.

Why not make a print of your foot on to a long envelope?

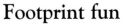

When the paint is dry you can write over the prints.

Footprint fun

Make your own personal stationery set by dipping your feet or hands into some paint and printing them on to some coloured paper and envelopes. This is messy, so it is a good idea to use washable paint, such as poster paint, and to put some plastic sheeting down first.

JOKE ATTACK

Mixed up amongst these jokes are some drawings that translate into words or phrases. Can you tell what they are? (Answers are on page 61).

Why are vampires artistic? Because they're good at drawing blood!

HO HO

Shall I tell you the joke about the pencil? No, there's no point in it!

1

2

TEE HEE

3

What did the oil painting say to the wall? First you framed me, then you hung me!

HA HA HA

40

HA HA HA

What is the best way to get paint off a chair?

Sit on it before the paint's dry!

Why are art galleries like retirement homes for teachers?

Because they're both full of old masters!

TEE HEE

HO HO HO

Doctor! Doctor! I keep feeling the urge to colour myself in gold paint!

You must have a gilt complex!

KRISS KROSS

Do you know someone who loves playing noughts and crosses? Why not present them with their own colourful giant-sized set?

From nought to crosses

Materials

Newspaper

Kitchen towel

Sticky tape   Paint

PVA glue

Scissors

Paintbrush

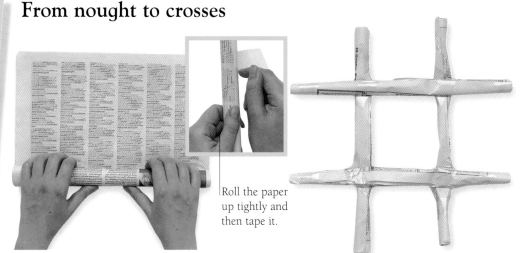

Roll the paper up tightly and then tape it.

1 Take a double page of newspaper and fold it in half. Roll it into a tube and then tape it in place. Make three more of these paper tubes.

2 Position your paper tubes to form a playing grid. Then fasten the tubes together using sticky tape.

Twist the rolled paper between your hands.

3 Next, take another folded sheet of paper and twist it tightly from bottom to top. Make ten of these.

Tape the two paper pieces together to form a cross. Do this five times to make five crosses.

4 Take one of the twisted pieces of newspaper and hold it diagonally across the centre square of the playing grid. Cut off a piece to fit in the square. Do this twice and tape the two pieces together.

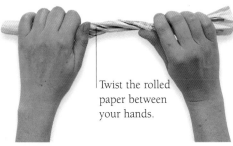

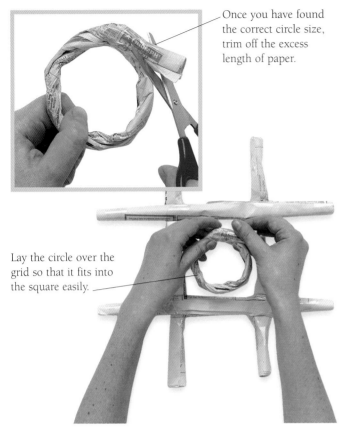

Once you have found the correct circle size, trim off the excess length of paper.

Lay the circle over the grid so that it fits into the square easily.

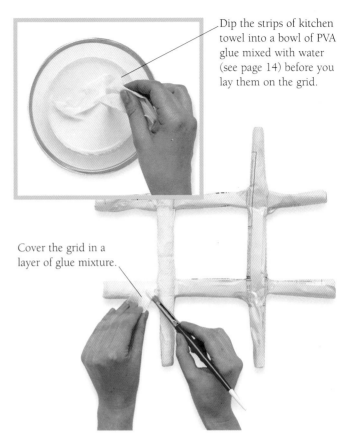

Dip the strips of kitchen towel into a bowl of PVA glue mixed with water (see page 14) before you lay them on the grid.

Cover the grid in a layer of glue mixture.

5 Curl another length of twisted paper into a circle. Position it over the playing grid to measure the correct size of the circle. Tape it together and trim off the excess. Do this five times to form five circles.

6 With a brush, spread some glue mixture over the grid. Add some strips of kitchen towel. Cover the whole grid with the strips and then add a second layer of glue mixture and kitchen towel.

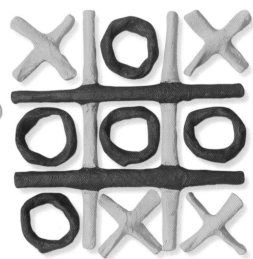

Make sure the noughts and crosses do not touch the grid or they might stick.

7 Next cover the noughts and crosses in layers of glue mixture and kitchen towel. Place them in the grid and leave the model to dry overnight.

8 Then colour all the noughts and crosses and the grid in two different colours using acrylic or poster paints. Leave them to dry.

KRISS KROSS

If you want a noughts and crosses set that is special, why not make it multi-coloured or even replace your crosses with clay creatures?

Be careful to make pieces that fit into the grid.

Paint tip
Make sure you leave the first colour to dry before you paint on the spots.

Paint your pieces in bold, contrasting colours.

Polka dots
The good thing about these noughts and crosses is that you can paint them in your favourite colours. Or you can make them exciting by adding polka dots or stripes.

You could paint your pieces with stripes instead of these spots.

Make sure you leave your clay pieces to harden before you paint them.

Pandas and zebras
If you want an alternative to noughts and crosses, you can make pandas and zebras or any animals you like out of modelling clay. Then all you do is give them a coat of paint!

Paint the grid in spots or stripes to complement your animal faces.

You can give all your animal faces different expressions.

Use a thin brush to paint on the facial features and stripes.

IT'S A-MAZE-ING

HELP!

Neil has been separated from his Art Attack equipment. Can you help him find his way

through the maze? Then try and find letters in the hedges to spell out "Art Attack".

47

TIME FRAME

Hww would you like to construct a colourful calendar that also doubles up as a frame for snapshots of your family and friends?

From discs to dials

Materials

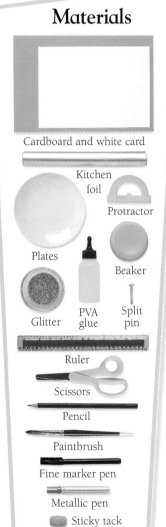

Cardboard and white card
Kitchen foil
Protractor
Plates
Beaker
Glitter
PVA glue
Split pin
Ruler
Scissors
Pencil
Paintbrush
Fine marker pen
Metallic pen
Sticky tack

Make a frame at least 3 cm wide.

1 Take two pieces of thick cardboard. Draw a large circle on each using a dinner plate. Then cut the two circles out.

2 Put a smaller plate or dish in the centre of one of the circles and draw around it. Cut it out making sure the frame stays in one piece.

Snip the edge of the foil so that it folds over easily without tearing.

Overlap each piece of foil as you stick it down.

3 Glue the frame to the dull side of a sheet of kitchen foil. Trim the foil to within 2.5 cm of the frame edge. Fold it over and glue it to the cardboard.

4 To make the backboard of the frame, glue one side of the other circle and cover it in foil. Fold the foil over the edges and glue it down.

Cut out a small frame about 1.5 cm wide.

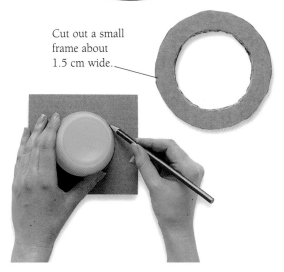

Place your small frame onto the cardboard to use as a guide for finding the size of the numbers.

Cover the numbers in silver foil.

5
Using an upside-down beaker, draw two circles on cardboard and cut them out. Draw two more circles inside these ones using the beaker the right way up. Cut these smaller circles out to leave two frames about 1.5 cm wide.

6
Draw the numbers one and two on some cardboard, roughly the same height and width as the small frames. Cut them out. Then brush all the numbers with glue and cover them with foil.

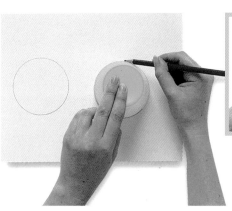

Use a ruler or compass to find the centre of each cardboard circle.

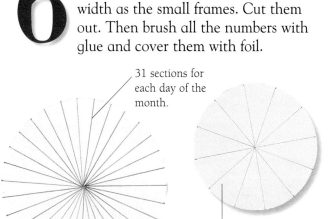

31 sections for each day of the month.

Divide this circle in 12 sections for each month of the year.

7
To make the dials, take the same beaker used in step 5 and draw around its rim on to some white card. Cut out two circles. Use a ruler to find the centre of each card circle.

8
Using a protractor, divide one circle into 31 sections, about 11.6° apart, and the other into 12 sections, 30° apart. Get an adult to help you. Mark out the sections by drawing lines out from the centre of the circle with a ruler.

Just write the first three letters of each month.

9
Place the small frames over the dials. Draw a fine pencil line along each inner edge. Under this line, write in numbers 1 to 31 for the days on one dial, and the names of each month on the other.

10
Placing some sticky tack underneath to protect the table, make a hole with a pencil in the centre of each dial. Then, cut out an arrow about 2.5 cm long from some card and colour it with a silver metallic pen.

Make a hole in the arrow with a pencil.

49

TIME FRAME

Just turn the dials to show the date and month of the year. Or if you're interested in the weather, make another time frame to indicate the seasons.

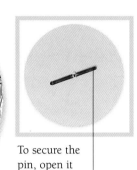

Split-pin tip
You may want to get an adult to help you when you push the split pin through the cardboard.

Sprinkle your frames with glitter.

Rub out the pencil guidelines on the dials.

To secure the pin, open it out at the back.

11
To decorate your calendar frame, spread some PVA glue on to the main frame, small frames, and numbers. Sprinkle them with a thick layer of glitter and shake off the excess.

12
Glue the small frames on to the dials. Then lay the arrow in the centre of each dial, lining up the holes. Next push a split pin through the holes and open them out at the back.

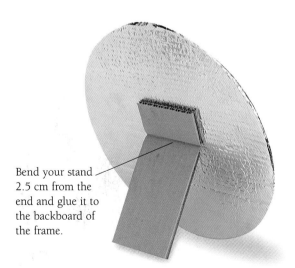

Bend your stand 2.5 cm from the end and glue it to the backboard of the frame.

Turn the dials to the correct date.

Stick your photos or pictures on to the backboard.

Stick the frame over your photos or pictures.

13
From cardboard, cut out a stand 15 cm long. Then make a bend 2.5 cm from the end and stick it to the backboard of the picture frame.

14
Stick your photos or pictures on to the plain side of the backboard. Glue the main frame over the top. Finally, stick the dials and numbers on to the main frame to form the date 2001.

Ship wreck

Why not paint a fantasy scene, such as this tropical island beach, on the backboard? Then you can cut out photos of your friends and stick them on the top to make your frame really fun. You could even take photos especially to go on your scene.

Use poster or acrylic paints to draw an exotic scene on to your time frame.

Star burst

Instead of making dials that show the date, why not make some season and weather dials? Just divide the dials into four seasons and four types of weather. You can change the weather dial when you get up each morning.

Why not get your friends to dress up in costume for your picture?

All the family

You could even make a simple photo collage so that you have lots of family and friends in your frame at the same time. Don't forget to include your pets!

Paint a cheerful sun to greet you every morning.

Why not colour your frame to match your bedroom?

BUG FOIL PLAQUE

Kitchen foil is a great art material, and you don't need a lot to create a dramatic Art Attack. Try designing one of these foil plaques!

From foil to plaque

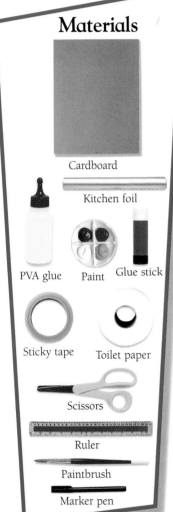

Materials

Cardboard

Kitchen foil

PVA glue   Paint   Glue stick

Sticky tape   Toilet paper

Scissors

Ruler

Paintbrush

Marker pen

Plaque border

1 Cut out two pieces of cardboard, roughly 20 cm by 15 cm. Take one of the pieces and draw a 1 cm border around the edge.

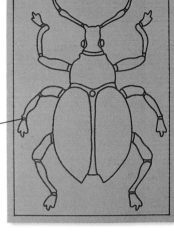

Draw thick lines to make them easy to see when you are cutting out.

2 Use a marker pen or pencil to draw your insect inside the border, making sure it fills the whole area. Then cut out the border in one piece.

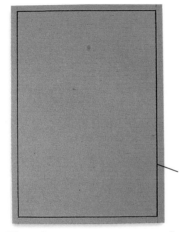

Draw an outline for each section as a cutting out guide.

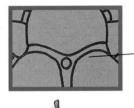

3 Divide your picture into small sections, as shown here. Cut out each section carefully, and glue it in position in the centre on the second piece of cardboard.

Snout beetle

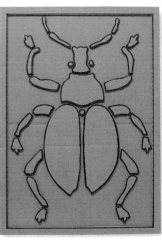

4 Next, cover one side of your border with some glue and stick it to the front of your plaque. Make sure that the border matches up with the edge of the plaque and fits neatly round the edge of your picture.

5 Brush your plaque with PVA glue and cover it with kitchen foil. Press down into the nooks and crannies with some toilet paper. Fold the edges of the foil over the back of the plaque and tape it down.

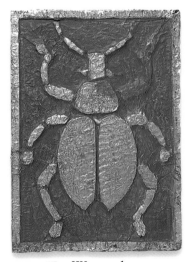

6 Water down some poster paint and brush it over the whole picture. Then take a piece of toilet paper and carefully wipe off the wet paint from the raised parts of the picture.

Creepy crawly beetle
And here it is, your very own kitchen-foil plaque. Add some extra detail to brighten up the picture, by lightly applying different colours to the silver areas when the plaque is dry. Have a go!

Number tip
If you number the sections of your bug picture before you cut them out it will help you reposition them later.

THE BIG ART ATTACK

I'm at a seaside fair which gives me a brilliant idea for a Big Art Attack . . .

1 Starting out
A gift shop is a great place to start. It's full of all sorts of items, big and small, that will be really handy for the picture.

2 Ducking and diving
Now what have we here – a yellow rubber duck, a spade, and flippers. I wonder which one of these I should use in my picture?

3 A day at the seaside
After a while, my seaside materials are gathered into a pile and I'm ready to start putting them into place.

The camera operator has to film me, so I stop from time to time.

4 Camera close-up
We shoot a lot of close-ups while I am laying down the materials. These shots help to keep you guessing what the final picture will be!

5 Bird's-eye view
Every now and then I need to stand back and check how the picture is coming along, so I take a look at what the overhead camera can see.

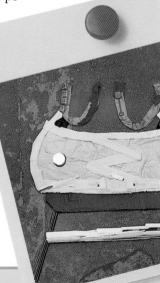

6 Coming along
Now that I've seen the picture from above I know exactly where to place the next lot of bits and pieces.

7 Checkpoint
Time for another check from above, and I think it's looking pretty good! I suspect that you'll be able to guess what it is by now.

8 The smallest detail
OK, so I'm nearly there – it just needs the finishing touches. Even the tiny things make a huge difference to the final picture.

The second camera operator always takes an overhead shot from a crane.

9 Ta-da!
So, here it is! I always stand next to the big Art Attack so you can see how big the picture is.

It's very difficult to tell what items I have used when the picture is finished!

DESK SET

Do you have a desk that always seems to be untidy? Why not create a family of froggies to help keep your desk in order?

From clay to frog

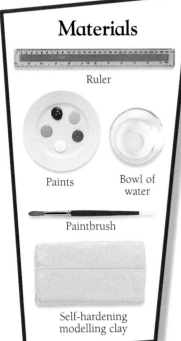

Materials

Ruler

Paints

Bowl of water

Paintbrush

Self-hardening modelling clay

1 Take two lumps of clay, one large, one small. Roll the larger piece into a ball and flatten the bottom so that it is stable. Press a paintbrush into the clay to make a deep groove.

This will be the frog's mouth.

Flatten the smaller ball of clay with the palm of your hand.

Clay tip
If your clay begins to dry out, sprinkle some water on to it so that you can mould it more easily.

2 Roll the smaller clay piece into a ball. Squash it with your palm. With a ruler cut the clay in half vertically. Make a horizontal cut about $\frac{2}{3}$ of the way up.

Make small indentations with the end of your brush.

3 To create a webbed feet effect, use the end of a brush to mark small indentations around the edge of the clay. You now have the front and back feet.

4 Hold the ball of clay in the palm of your hand. Turn it over so that it shows the flat side, with the mouth side furthest from you. Brush some water on to the flat surface.

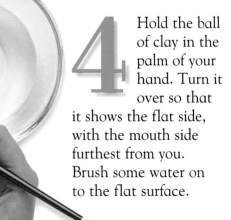

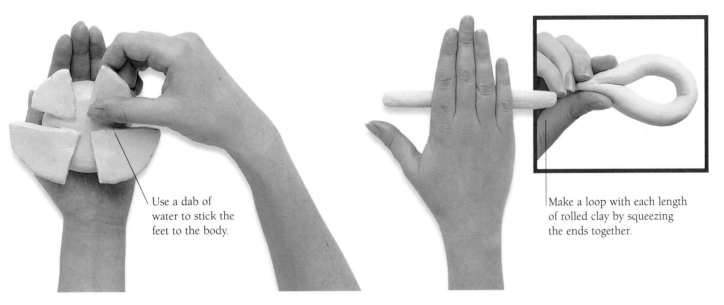

Use a dab of water to stick the feet to the body.

Make a loop with each length of rolled clay by squeezing the ends together.

5 Take the two big feet and lay them on the back of the frog, so they stick out each side. Then, lay the two small feet underneath the mouth area. Carefully, turn the frog back over and leave it to dry.

6 Take another piece of clay and roll it into a sausage a bit longer than a finger. Do this twice to make two long, thin sausage-shaped clay strips. Bend them over to make two loops.

7 To form the frog's back legs, wet the pinched ends of the clay loops and place them in the space between the back feet and the body. Use a paintbrush to help you press them into place. Then, roll two more balls of clay to form the frog's eyes.

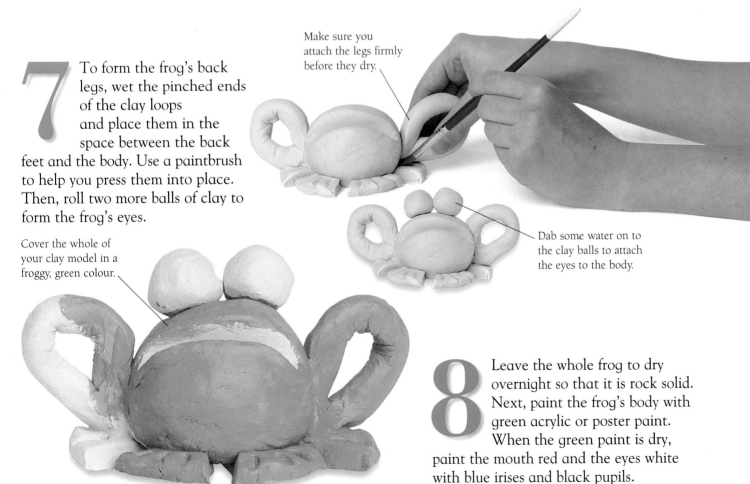

Make sure you attach the legs firmly before they dry.

Dab some water on to the clay balls to attach the eyes to the body.

Cover the whole of your clay model in a froggy, green colour.

8 Leave the whole frog to dry overnight so that it is rock solid. Next, paint the frog's body with green acrylic or poster paint. When the green paint is dry, paint the mouth red and the eyes white with blue irises and black pupils.

DESK SET

Your frogs are now ready for a makeover! Experiment with lots of colours, and if you like, adapt your frog into a fish or any other creature you like.

The blue irises and black pupils bring your frog to life.

Paint the inside of the mouth a bright red.

Green alert

When you have coloured the frog's body green, you can add some yellow spots to give the frog more character. Once your frog is painted, place a paintbrush or pen into the frog's mouth. It's a handy place to keep your desk items.

Make the frog's eyes shine by adding triangular highlights.

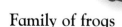

MADE IN ENGLAND

You can place long or short rulers into the frog's mouth.

Family of frogs

Make a family of frogs in different colours so that your desk top looks really colourful.

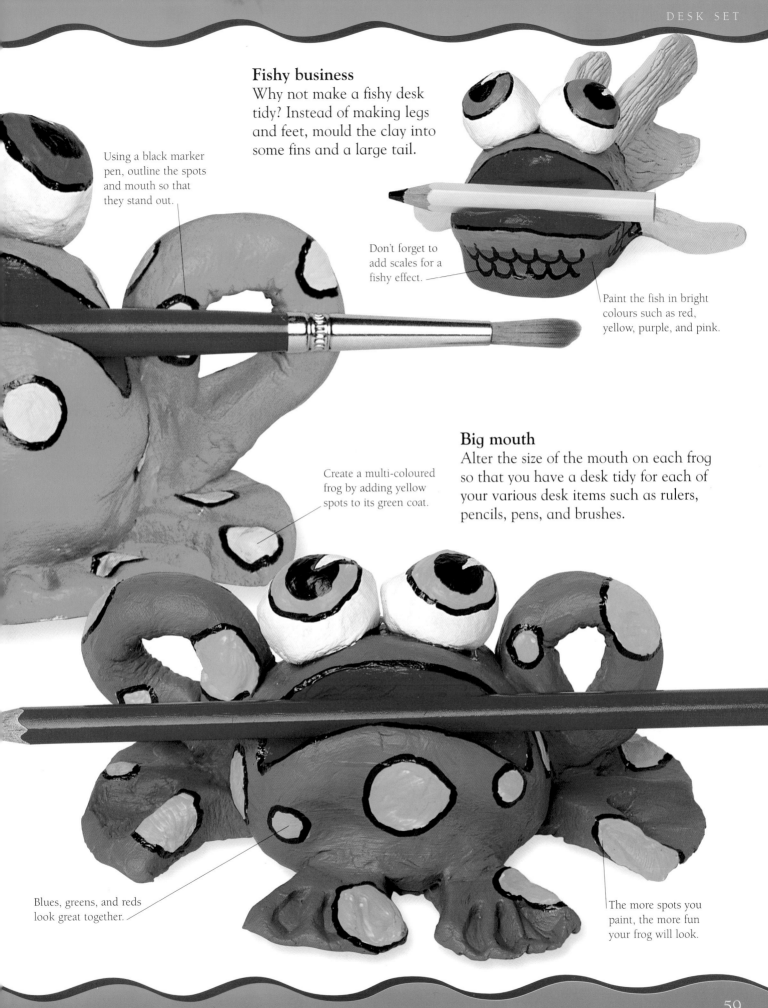

Fishy business
Why not make a fishy desk tidy? Instead of making legs and feet, mould the clay into some fins and a large tail.

Using a black marker pen, outline the spots and mouth so that they stand out.

Don't forget to add scales for a fishy effect.

Paint the fish in bright colours such as red, yellow, purple, and pink.

Create a multi-coloured frog by adding yellow spots to its green coat.

Big mouth
Alter the size of the mouth on each frog so that you have a desk tidy for each of your various desk items such as rulers, pencils, pens, and brushes.

Blues, greens, and reds look great together.

The more spots you paint, the more fun your frog will look.

INDEX

ANSWERS

Front inside jacket
Paintbrush puzzle: the yellow, spotted brush is the last one left on the board.

Pages 34-35 Puzzle Page
Big Art Attack word puzzle: you can find these words plus many more – at, attic, back, bag, bait, bar, bat, batik, bit, brat, cat, cart, crab, crag, gait, gib, grab, grit, it, kit, rag, rat, rib, rig, tab, tack, tag, tar, tick, trick.

Word search:

E	P I C A S S O	N	Y
S	R E N R U T	C	R	D
S	Z E I N B Y	W	Z	A
I	G B M C E O G	D	L
T	A R J B L K P E	I
A	Y D K O R M H G	B
M O N E T	U A F A	Z
V	Z B J P U W N S	C
X	V A N G O G H D	E
S B M W A R H O L T

Anagram: the letters, when unscambled, spell acrylic.
What is it? It's the frog desk tidy.

Crossword: Across: 1. Papier 4. Pen 5. Neil 6. Art 7. Frame 10. Indigo 13. Yes; **Down:** 1. Poster 2. Pencil 3. Ruler 4. PVA 7. Frog 8. Mix 9. Brush 10. Ink 11. Dot 12. Oil.
Paint Pot Puzzle: the colours are purple, crimson, pink, and violet.

Pages 40-41 Joke Attack
The pictures translate into these words: 1. spring onion 2. dormouse 3. tin of peas 4. two Mexicans on a bike 5. running tap 6. giraffe walking past a window 7. person stuck in a lift 8. spider on a mirror 9. orange squash

Back inside jacket
Palette puzzle: white and black paints = grey; white and red paints = pink; yellow and blue paints = green; yellow and blue and red paints = brown; red and blue paints = purple; red and yellow paints = orange.

ACKNOWLEDGMENTS

Dorling Kindersley would like to thank the following people for their help in the production of this book: Suzanne Garton for making Art Attack material available; Penny York, Caroline Greene, and Lee Simmons for editorial assistance; Robin Hunter for computer graphics; Lynn Bresler for the index; Chloe Smith for modelling her hands and feet.